"Marcia has challenged and inspired me with her devotionals over the years. What a blessing she has been to my life!"

Gina Holmes, best-selling author
Crossing Oceans, Dry as Rain, Wings of Glass, and *Driftwood Tides.*

Abundant Rain

A DEVOTIONAL JOURNAL FOR
WRITERS OF FAITH, VOLUME 1
(REVISED EDITION)

MARCIA LEE LAYCOCK

Published by Siretona Creative. www.siretona.com

978-1-998249-29-9 Electronic
978-1-998249-32-9 Paperback

Cover and interior design: Colleen McCubbin
Cover art: Adobe Stock
Font: Albertan Pro Book

Distributed to the trade by Ingram Book Company.

*Let my teaching fall like rain
and my words descend like dew,
like showers on new grass,
like abundant rain on tender plants.*

Deuteronomy 32:2

CONTENTS

A BAG OF FISH OR JESUS

After his resurrection, Jesus told the disciples what to do, and where to go, but they doubted Him. One of their leaders, an impetuous fellow named Peter, said, "I'm going fishing." The others said, "Yeah, sounds like a good idea."

We are all prone to oh—so—quickly give up on God and turn back to our own resources, just as the disciples did. They fished for hours to no avail. When a man turned up on the shore and asked if they had any fish, they all shouted a resounding, "No!"

It's after that man told them to cast their net on the other side of their boat that John said, "Hey—uh—I think maybe it's Jesus."

To his credit, Peter wasted no more time with the fish—he hurried to shore. Then Jesus, who was indeed the one speaking, told them to bring some of the fish they'd just caught to the fire. An interesting statement, that. Jesus already had fish roasting over the coals, yet he directed them to bring what they had just caught with their own hands.

There are a couple of lessons to learn here. One, guard against giving up on God. He will come through, He's never late, and He will always give us what we need to accomplish what He has in mind. Two, there's a principle to learn from Peter and the disciples. We can so easily get caught up in striving to make a living—trying to make things work out the way we want—that we can lose sight of the One for whom we are working. But as Peter discovered, when Jesus shows up, the bag of fish is suddenly of no importance. Being with Jesus is all that matters.

There's a third principle to learn: we can know God intends to put us to work. He has given us skills—like the ability to catch fish and write books or poetry or magazine articles—and He will use those skills to His own purposes. Part of that purpose is to teach us and bless us abundantly, as we become a blessing to others. The disciples ate as much fish as they wanted that morning and had plenty left to sell. It was the fruit of their own labour, but it was labour guided by their Lord, labour that taught them something about Him, labour that was indeed life—giving.

"So, whatever you do, work at it with all your heart, as working for the Lord, not for men, since you know that you will receive an inheritance from the Lord as a reward. It is the Lord Christ you are serving" (Colossians 3:23).

How can you ensure that you are staying close to Jesus as you write?

_____
_____
_____
_____
_____
_____
_____
_____
_____
_____
_____
_____
_____
_____
_____
_____
_____
_____
_____
_____
_____
_____
_____
_____
_____

A DIVINE APPOINTMENT

"Do you know anything about these flowers?"

The young woman's eyes were hopeful, but I had to disappoint her and explain that I did not work in the hospital gift shop, I was just there to stock the book rack. I pointed to two ladies at a nearby counter. "Maybe they can help," I said.

She nodded, stared at the flower display, and sighed. "I'm not really sure what I want."

I took note of her clothing then—a baseball cap pulled over messy hair, a thin pair of pajama bottoms topped by a hospital issue housecoat wrapped around a frail frame, pull-on terrycloth slippers, two sizes too big.

"My friend is dying," she said, then turned back to me. "I am too."

I put my clipboard down and waited. Her story unfolded in simple language, the words slipping from her mouth almost as though rehearsed. She reached into a pocket and pulled out a picture of her seven-year-old daughter. I could see the resemblance. She smiled when I mentioned it and went on to say there was a surgery that she was hoping for—highly experimental, there was only one doctor who could do it and he just happened to live in a nearby city. But then her voice fell, and I had to lean close to hear. Her friend had had the surgery. She was still dying.

The conversation turned to the word hope then. She had hope they would agree to do the surgery, hope that, unlike her friend, she would recover, hope that she would live to watch her daughter grow up.

She said a pastor came to visit sometimes. "We say our small prayers together. They seem small, just words, but maybe not, eh?" Again, that hopeful look in her eyes.

I was praying small prayers right then. *She's so young, Lord. Please. Please.*

Then she was gone, and I resumed stocking the rack. I used to it once a month, and in that hospital the rack was usually almost empty by the time I returned. As I filled the pockets with books, I was acutely aware of their contents. They hold pages about the love and mercy of Jesus, pages filled with stories of courage and faith, pages of humour to lift a sad heart, and inspiration to encourage a weary soul. Pages of hope.

I knew I was sent there that day to do much more than "just stock the book racks," but my job suddenly seemed important. My other job, as a writer, suddenly seemed essential, "That I may publish with the voice of thanksgiving, and tell of all thy wondrous works" (Psalm 26:7, KJV).

What Divine appointments have you had
that encouraged you in your writing?

_____

_____

_____

_____

_____

_____

_____

_____

_____

_____

_____

_____

_____

_____

_____

_____

_____

_____

_____

_____

_____

_____

A FAITHFUL "NO"

Thinking about selling books, I clicked into a local church's website to see if there were anything events coming up. I was hoping they might allow me to set up a book table. I was glad to see there was an event very soon, so I e-mailed the woman in charge with my idea.

She e-mailed back, but the answer was no. The committee thought it might be too much of a distraction. That did not brighten my mood. Other doors had closed that week and, as I looked at the total number of books I had managed to sell in the past year, I became discouraged. I sat at my computer that day and thought maybe I should just quit.

But I went to the event. It was a live video feed with a well-known speaker. As I walked into the sanctuary that Friday evening, I wasn't feeling in the mood—I was still angry and frustrated and, underneath, wondered why God wasn't helping me to get the word out about my books. The video began and I found it did nothing to help. The sound was a bit wobbly and the music seemed "canned." I thought, *Oh yeah, here we go with another hyped-up performance that will leave me cold.*

Then the speaker began. Slowly her passion and sincerity broke through. Her humour lifted the heaviness, and I began to listen for what God was saying to me. He said plenty. Then the worship group came back on, and suddenly the music lifted me into that place of praise and worship. By the end of the evening I was in tears at God's wonderful grace and mercy and unconditional love. I felt ashamed at my lack of trust.

The next day was more of the same. I don't think it was a coincidence that the message was from Luke 8, which lays out the parable of the sower and talks about those who hear but don't respond, those who fall away in "the time of testing," and those who "hear, but as they go on their way they are choked by life's worries, riches and pleasures and they do not mature."

I left that place with a renewed sense of how alive my God is, how good, and how faithful. Best of all, I had a renewed passion for His Word—something that has been lacking in my life for a while. And I was so glad for that faithful 'no.' Had I been concerned with selling books I would have been distracted from what God wanted to say to me. I might not have heard Him at all.

As I read the rest of Luke 8 at home later, verse 18 popped out: "Therefore consider carefully how you listen." That's a verse to which I think we can all say, "Amen!"

Have you ever had a faithful "No?"

_____

_____

_____

_____

_____

_____

_____

_____

_____

_____

_____

_____

_____

_____

_____

_____

_____

_____

_____

_____

_____

_____

_____

_____

_____

A FEW GOOD QUESTIONS

A writer/editor I greatly respect wrote, "We need to keep our own fallibility very much in mind, adopting a humble posture towards the readers we serve and God, whom we seek to honour" (Doug Koop, editor, *Christian Week Newspaper*).

Mr. Koop says there are some questions we need to ask ourselves, as writers.

Do they [our words] encourage better attitudes? Do they inspire better activity? Do they edify? Do they entertain? Do they strengthen the right muscles? Do they inform truthfully and graciously? Do they honour Jesus Christ and the Church He loves? Those kinds of questions matter ...

As I read his column, it gave me pause. Can I put a checkmark beside each of those questions when I consider my work? I would hope so. I think Mr. Koop has encapsulated what it means to be a writer who is Christian, both in terms of motivation and practice.

It is a high calling, one not to be taken lightly, one not to be used to grow our own egos, but to act as the conduit for God's purposes. He has purposes for our words—purposes that involve people we may never meet—a young woman who needs emotional healing, a young man who needs to deal with his anger, an elderly woman who needs to forgive, an elderly man who just needs a good laugh.

All we have to do is keep in step with God's Spirit, guard our hearts so that our perspective on our work always falls within the realm of humility, and trust Him to guide us in our lives and in our work.

All we have to do is respect our readers enough to work hard at finding the right words, praying they will understand and act upon the words we write, and honour God enough to acknowledge His sovereignty as He does with them what He will.

Our words, used to God's purposes, can affect change in the lives of our readers. All we have to do is choose them wisely, put them together with skill and attention to detail, and then get out of the way.

For "of this gospel I was appointed a herald" (2 Timothy 1:11).

How are you guarding your heart?

_____

_____

_____

_____

_____

_____

_____

_____

_____

_____

_____

_____

_____

_____

_____

_____

_____

_____

_____

_____

_____

_____

_____

_____

_____

A LESSON FROM POMPEII

The television screen flashed with images of human forms frozen forever in the throes of death. A man slumped forward, knees pulled to his chest, his face buried in his hands. Two skeletons were entangled in a lover's embrace. A mother clutched her child. The people of Pompeii.

The documentary gave a dramatic rendition of what the last days and hours of that city may have been like, as the volcano rumbled and then erupted. The program was fascinating and chilling. I was especially struck by a scene in which a family prayed fervently before the shrines of their Roman gods—gods that could neither hear nor help them.

It's perhaps tempting for us to think we would never do such a thing, never depend on that which is powerless to help us. Yet we do it all the time.

Writers are especially guilty, I fear, as we get wrapped up in marketing hype and the advice of 'experts' who tell us we must bow at the altars of 'platform' and 'social networking.' All of us know such things are of use, and even necessary to a successful career. But what do they really give us for all our effort? They may result in more book sales—or not. They may make our name known in wider circles—or not. More books sold is an empty end if lives are not changed. The fame of our name is pointless if it is not connected to the only Name that matters.

I like to think of my work is terms of sowing seeds that God can use to change lives. In order for that to happen I need to be bowing before God's altar, worshipping in spirit and in truth. I need to ensure that His Spirit is flowing through me, into the words typed into my computer. I need to be relying on Him and Him alone to accomplish all that He ordains for my work.

And I need to mean it. Mean it with all my heart and soul, mean it to the point of weeping for my readers. This idea hit me recently when I read a scripture I've read many times before: "Those who sow in tears shall reap in joy" (Psalm 126:5, NKJV).

I confess I'm not there yet. I haven't wept for the salvation of my readers, nor for the healing of their emotional hurts. But I want to be there. I want to care as much as Jesus does. But it's hard. A lot of distractions get in the way. Things like platforms and social networks. So I keep praying for those moments when tears do fall as I write, and the groanings of my heart have to be translated by His Spirit. Then I take heart with scriptures like this: "And let us not be weary in well-doing: for in due season we shall reap, if we faint not" (Galatians 6:9, KJV).

Have you ever wept for your readers?

_____

_____

_____

_____

_____

_____

_____

_____

_____

_____

_____

_____

_____

_____

_____

_____

_____

_____

_____

_____

_____

_____

_____

_____

A LIFE WORTHY

I once had to walk through a swamp with a heavy pack on my back. I stumbled at almost every step because of the muskeg, my legs chilled to the bone by ice-cold water that lurked beneath the hummocks of grass I tried to walk on. It was an exhausting effort, and I almost turned back, but I had a friend with me who continually turned and encouraged me with words that made me believe I could do what had to be done. I finished that arduous trip only because I sensed that he believed I could do it and it made me want to.

In Ephesians 4:1, the Apostle Paul writes, "I urge you to live a life worthy of the calling you have received." On the one hand this makes me smile and want to step forward with my head held high. On the other hand, it makes me cringe.

As Christians we have received a primary calling to be like Jesus and to glorify Him in all things. That calling is irrevocable. And I am painfully aware that I fail to be worthy of it every day. I continually fall into sinful attitudes and thoughts, let alone actions. It makes me think of Paul's cry in Romans: "Oh wretched man that I am!" He too knew himself to be weak and unworthy, in his flesh, yet he also says, "Although I am less that the least of all God's people, this grace was given me: to preach to the Gentiles the unsearchable riches of Christ" (Ephesians 3:8).

And in that I am encouraged, because the calling on my life does not depend on my worthiness. It depends only on God's grace and that will always be sufficient for the task, not so that I will succeed, not so that others will praise me, but so that the name of Christ will be exalted.

How amazing that God chooses to use us, chooses to give us a calling and the grace with which to accomplish it! Such awareness causes me to strive to do what Paul admonished the Ephesians to do—live a life worthy of the name God has bestowed on us. How amazing that even though we fail, God continues to extend that calling and that grace, just as a coach continues to encourage his protégés even though they fall short of the mark time and again.

The encouragement is, in itself, sustaining, because just knowing that He doesn't give up on us keeps us going, keeps us striving, keeps us longing to live a life worthy—worthy of Him.

It is a journey that knows no limits, because it is one He designed, one He will see us through. All the way to eternity.

Reflect on this:
The calling on your life does not depend on your worthiness.

_____

_____

_____

_____

_____

_____

_____

_____

_____

_____

_____

_____

_____

_____

_____

_____

_____

_____

_____

_____

_____

_____

_____

_____

A LITTLE HELP FROM A FRIEND

When my daughter decided to take a language course by correspondence, I had some misgivings. Would she have the self-discipline to do the work and to complete it? Could she really learn a language by listening to audio recordings and reading a book? She dove in with enthusiasm at first, but quickly got bogged down. I did my best to encourage her to keep going.

We were working on an assignment together one morning when she looked up and said, "You know, Mom, I really want to know how to speak Spanish. I just don't want to have to learn it!"

I often thought of that day since then. It had been a struggle to get my next novel finished. I so wanted it to be finished. I dreamed of seeing the book in my hands and on the shelves of many bookstores. But at the time, I had little of the enthusiasm I needed for writing it.

Most writers hit this wall, when you have to force yourself to sit in the chair and do it. I had hit this point before and I knew it would pass. Like my daughter, I would persevere and the book would be written. I just had to get over this hump.

Sometimes the path of our spiritual life can have a lot of humps. We want to go to church but can't drum up the needed energy to get out the door. We want to read the Bible, but there are so many distractions. Even the Apostle Paul seems to have had a number of humps along the way. Hear his distress in these words,

So I find this law at work: When I want to do good, evil is right there with me. For in my inner being I delight in God's law; but I see another law at work in the members of my body, waging war against the law of my mind and making me a prisoner of the law of sin at work within my members. What a wretched man I am! Who will rescue me from this body of death? (Romans 7:20-24).

The struggle to live as we should, to enjoy God as He intended us to do, is sometimes more than a hump. It can seem like a mountain.

But listen to what Paul says next: "Thanks be to God through Jesus Christ our Lord!" (verse 25).

Paul made it over the hump, with a little help from a friend. The good news is He's our friend too and He's very good at bulldozing the humps in our lives, both spiritually and physically. He cares about all of it and he wants to help. Just ask Him.

What humps and mountains have you run into lately?

_____

_____

_____

_____

_____

_____

_____

_____

_____

_____

_____

_____

_____

_____

_____

_____

_____

_____

_____

_____

_____

_____

_____

_____

A MATTER OF TIMING

Last week I watched two geese land on a pond across from my home. It was funny to watch, because the pond was frozen. The geese gracefully flapped their wings and extended their feet, anticipating the landing, but when they touched down they skidded sideways and plopped down on their bottoms. When they recovered, they stomped about, seeming indignant.

When I watched them stomping around it made me think of those times when I've been impatient with God's timing. It often seems that He isn't in sync with my estimation of when things should happen. Give me patience, Lord. Right now!

But His timing is always perfect. When my new novel, *One Smooth Stone*, won the Best New Canadian Christian Author Award, I was thrilled that it would soon be in print. Then I discovered that the word "soon" is relative. There was a delay because the publisher wanted a certain editor to work with me, and she was busy with other projects. Then there was a bit of miscommunication—I was waiting for her while she was waiting for me to get in touch. Then, when it was finally begun, the editing process took time. But finally, my publisher told me the books were ready to ship. I waited—impatiently—for them to arrive on my doorstep. The book launch was to be held on the first night of a writers' conference and I wanted them in hand for that event. I was thankful when they arrived, safe and sound, a few days before.

I remember lifting the first book out of the box. I knew exactly where it was going. I gave it to my friend—I'll call her Barb.

Barb has had a hard life—her husband left her with four small children to raise and no resources. The family struggled through. Then one of Barb's daughters, I'll call her Lucy, was raped when she was a teenager. Though Barb managed to hold on to her faith in Christ, Lucy has been bitter and angry with God ever since. The day after my books arrived, Barb gave that copy of *One Smooth Stone* to Lucy. A few days later she got a phone call.

Lucy told her that she had had no intention of reading the book. But that next day she got the flu and the only thing she had in the house to read was my book. So she picked it up and started to read. She said she couldn't put it down. When she called her mom, she was in tears because she said that after reading the book, she finally believed God does still love her, in spite of everything.

The timing was perfect. God's timing. Not mine. Next time I get impatient I'll try and remember how ridiculous those geese looked, stomping around on solid ice.

Have you ever found yourself stomping on solid ice?

_____

_____

_____

_____

_____

_____

_____

_____

_____

_____

_____

_____

_____

_____

_____

_____

_____

_____

_____

_____

_____

_____

_____

_____

_____

A PACK RAT'S EPIPHANY

Moving day was fast approaching and it was time to declutter and organize my office before boxing it all up. I am an unrepentant pack rat, but I was amazed at what I had accumulated. I had piles of old copies of old articles to sort, some that had been published, some not. I had a box of writers' magazines, another of magazines in which friends had been published, and one of miscellaneous clippings. There were copies of my own work and editing projects I'd done for others. On and on and on. And then I opened my closet!

I stared at a box on the top shelf. I knew what it held and winced when I lifted it down. It contained an old green folder holding a manuscript handwritten on yellow newsprint. I wrote it during a long cold winter in a cabin in the Yukon many years ago. I should have thrown it away at least three moves previous to this one, but I just couldn't do it. It had "sentimental value," after all. It was the first book-length manuscript I had finished.

I carefully lifted the green cover. A musty smell wafted around me, and I remembered the long-ago day when I had first packed it up. That cabin had had a mouse problem for a while. Apparently, they liked yellow newsprint. The edges of the folder were gnawed. Part of the manuscript itself had a hole in it. When I lifted the sheets, some of it crumbled in my hand. But I had kept it, like a treasure, stored on the top shelf of that closet.

I glanced at the garbage pail, already almost full. I should toss it. I knew I should. But I'd spent months working on this story. I knew I'd never take the time to type it all out and work on it. I knew I would never send it to a publisher. I glanced at the garbage can again and hesitated.

Then I laughed at myself. Why did I value this rodent-chewed, smelly pile of paper so highly? I stood over the trash barrel and let the box, folder, and manuscript tumble in. Then a scripture came to mind—something about treasures and moths making holes in things. I found my Bible and looked it up: "but store up for yourselves treasures in heaven, where moth and rust [or rodents] do not destroy... For where your treasure is, there your heart will be also" (Matthew 6:19-21, parenthesis mine).

I went back to the garbage can, retrieved the box and opened the folder again. I lifted out a portion of the paper where a hungry little mouse had eaten through it. I found an old frame, placed the sheet between two pieces of glass and propped it up on the ledge by my computer. That I would pack, as a reminder to find more enduring treasures for my heart. The rest went back into the trash can.

What are you treasuring?

_____

_____

_____

_____

_____

_____

_____

_____

_____

_____

_____

_____

_____

_____

_____

_____

_____

_____

_____

_____

_____

_____

A PRIVILEGED POSITION

During a recent Bible study, we viewed part of a fascinating video called *The Privileged Planet* about a group of scientists and astronomers who wondered whether or not the earth is unique in the universe. They have uncovered some interesting facts.

Among other things, they concluded that the earth is uniquely positioned between two arms of the Milky Way so that we, its inhabitants, can observe the wonders of the universe. If our globe were in any other place in our solar system, not only would it be uninhabitable, the exploration of the space around us would not be possible. This is an intriguing detail that leads to the logical conclusion that the position of earth was not an accident.

As I watched that video, I realized that not only is the earth placed "just so," but its inhabitants are as well. Each one of us has been put in exactly the right spot to observe what is going on around us and to accomplish what God desires because of that observation. Writers are perhaps uniquely gifted in this endeavour. We seem to have an innate drive to observe and record. I've heard many writers say, "I can't help myself—I have to write about it."

I began to ponder the question "Why?" Why did God put the planet in just that spot? Why did He put me where I am, doing what I'm doing? The answer could lead me to the same conclusion those scientists reached, that I, like the planet, am indeed special in some way. And that would be astonishingly true, but I believe there is something more, something deeper to understand here.

Author and preacher John Piper helps us find the answer. He has said that everything is meant to glorify God. It's not about me. It's not about our planet. It's all about God bringing glory to Himself and, as Dr. Piper has said, "God is most glorified in us when we are most satisfied in Him." We are most satisfied in Him when we are doing what were created to do—drawing close to Him, getting to know Him more each day. Some of us have been called to do that through the process of writing. A privileged position indeed.

> Lord, you alone are my portion and my cup;
> you make my lot secure.
> The boundary lines have fallen for me in pleasant places;
> surely I have a delightful inheritance.
> I will praise the Lord, who counsels me;
> even at night my heart instructs me.
> I keep my eyes always on the Lord.

With him at my right hand, I will not be shaken.
Therefore my heart is glad and my tongue rejoices;
my body also will rest secure (Psalm 16:5-9).

Do you consider your inheritance as a writer delightful?

_____

_____

_____

_____

_____

_____

_____

_____

_____

_____

_____

_____

_____

_____

_____

_____

_____

_____

_____

_____

_____

_____

A SERMON JUST FOR ME

One Sunday, as I settled in my chair at church, I prayed a quick prayer. "Talk to me, Lord."

My husband tends to be a spontaneous person, and I've gotten used to him doing unexpected things. Sometimes. But that Sunday, he surprised me by announcing that I was going to give my testimony that morning, in three minutes or less. He hadn't warned me about this, probably because he didn't know he was going to do it until that very moment. As I walked up to the front I was thinking, *Good thing I'm good at public speaking.* The testimony part is a breeze, but in three minutes? No doubt he gave me a time limit, because he knows my tendency to go on and on. He did have a sermon to preach that morning. So I did what he asked, and all went well. As I expected it would.

Then my husband got up to preach. The sermon was on Mark 12:41-44, a short passage of scripture that seemed straightforward as he read it out loud. A poor widow gave all she had. She was extremely generous. She put the religious leaders to shame. But my husband, bless him, took a different tack when he said this little bit of scripture is really about pride and humility. *Huh?*

I felt God tapping me on the shoulder. I was feeling quite self-satisfied, having just given my testimony clearly, with just the right emphasis. In fact, I was thinking, *I really am good at that.* The more my favourite preacher spoke, the more I felt like crawling under my chair. I knew what had just happened was no coincidence.

God was talking to me, but I wasn't particularly happy to hear it.

Then my favourite preacher started talking about generosity. *Okay, that's better.* I sat up a bit. Then he said, "The core of generosity is humility." *Oh.* And he gave Neil T. Anderson's definition: "humility is confidence properly placed." *Oh dear.*

When Proverbs 29:23 appeared in big bold letters on the screen I had to grin just a little. "Pride brings you low." *Right. I really should remember that.*

I was encouraged when my husband acknowledged that he and everyone else in the room all struggle with pride. It's a big part of the human condition. The trick is to catch ourselves at it, repent of it, and put ourselves back in the place where we all need to be, at the feet of Jesus. Confidence properly placed. *Right. I definitely have to remember that.*

Do you struggle with pride as a writer?

_____

_____

_____

_____

_____

_____

_____

_____

_____

_____

_____

_____

_____

_____

_____

_____

_____

_____

_____

_____

_____

_____

_____

_____

_____

A SMALL PATCH OF BLUE

The day had been a fine drizzle of rain creating a thickening mist that shifted and swallowed all in its path. We were to drive to the high point on the Midnight Dome behind Dawson City, Yukon the next morning, and I prayed the morning sun would banish the fog and let us see the stunning view of the Klondike Valley. I hadn't seen it for many years, and I longed for the exhilaration it had always given me. But the next morning the fog lingered.

"Let's go up anyway," my husband said, "at least as far as the cemetery." I knew what he intended. The cemetery held the graves of two good friends, men in their twenties who had taken their own lives in a suicide pact many years before. Their deaths had been the catalyst for the journey to faith in Jesus. We wandered among the graves, noting names we recognized from years gone by. How young some of them had been when death claimed their mortal bodies.

We found the graves we were looking for—one marked by the idler wheel of a D6 Cat, the other by the front frame of a piece of heavy machinery. I watched as my husband pushed scrub brush away so we could see their names welded on the unusual headstones. Memories of that time brought a quietness to the place.

Neither of us wanted to head back, so we continued up the dirt road as it wound its way to the top. The peak of the Dome was above the clouds, so we looked down on the grey shifting mist, watching as it slowly began to dissipate. A small patch of blue appeared. Part of the Yukon River. I was puzzled when I saw it emerge. At this point in the river's course, the Yukon is not blue. It's a milky grey, filled with silt from a river upstream. Then I realized the river was reflecting the blue sky above, slowly being revealed as the clouds moved away.

I thought of all the people who had come into our lives at that time of death and tragedy, people who prayed with us and guided us toward the truth about life, death and eternity. And I smiled. They themselves were just ordinary people, living ordinary lives in an isolated place, but they reflected something from beyond themselves. Something that glowed with the colour of vibrancy and life—the face of God.

I pray that will be the case with everything I write. Though it may have little that is called extraordinary in its pages, though it may exist in a world filled with shifting fog, may it be a reflection of truth, flowing with the colour of true life, able to translate into healing, able to reflect the love of a holy God. May it draw my readers along, as that small patch of blue river below us did, to a place where they will meet Him and know Him, just a little bit more than they did before.

Is your writing like that small patch of blue?

_____
_____
_____
_____
_____
_____
_____
_____
_____
_____
_____
_____
_____
_____
_____
_____
_____
_____
_____
_____
_____
_____
_____
_____
_____

A SMALL PHRASE OF BEAUTY

The Canadian Oxford dictionary defines transcendent as "something beyond the grasp of human experience." My husband once defined it as "a tiny piece of wonder, a small phrase of beauty."

I've had a few of them, those tiny pieces of wonder. They have come in the midst of God's creation—standing on the edge of a cliff overlooking the vastness of Lake Superior, or in the middle of an evergreen forest as big flakes of snow fell in silence. I once experienced it on the shores of a small Alberta lake, watching a friend be baptized at sunset.

I've also experienced those small phrases of beauty when reading a different version of scripture than I would normally use. I found this in The Message: "learning the unforced rhythms of grace." And this one in the King James Version: "The waters are hid as with a stone and the face of the deep is frozen." I've found them in quotes on the internet and buried in counseling tomes. I've found them in books written by friends and strangers.

I experienced an unusual one recently on a very ordinary evening as ten or twelve people crowded into our living room to study the Gospel of John. Snacks were on the coffee table, along with a jug of juice, and people chatted as they helped themselves. Then, as everyone settled, my husband asked, "What do you wish for the place where you are right now? What do you envision for that place?" There was silence for a time, then one young man smiled. "Something fantastic!" he said, "Something explosive!"

I smiled at his exuberance. As God's word unfolded, I had a "tiny piece of wonder." I looked around at the faces of the people there and saw the shine of faith in their eyes. I saw their passion to know God more, their zeal to do what God asked of them, and I realized that this was something fantastic, something explosive, right here in our living room.

And that awareness lifted me above human experience, above the reality that our church is small and doesn't even have its own building, above the reality that less than ten percent of our community worships God on any given Sunday, let alone through the rest of the week. That moment of transcendence gave me a great deal of hope for this place where we are right now. It thrilled me to feel the presence of God there and to know that He has given us a part in His plan for this place. It filled me with gratitude and humbled me beyond words. Sometimes God opens our understanding and something ordinary becomes "a small phrase of beauty." We are lifted beyond our experience and we see with new eyes. Perhaps it happens because someone prayed, as the Apostle Paul did, "that the eyes of your heart may be enlightened in order that you may know the hope to which he has called you, the riches of his glorious inheritance in the saints, and his incomparably great power for us who believe" (Ephesians 1:18-19).

Have you ever experienced a moment of transcendence?

_____

_____

_____

_____

_____

_____

_____

_____

_____

_____

_____

_____

_____

_____

_____

_____

_____

_____

_____

_____

_____

_____

A WORTHY GOAL, A PRECIOUS PRIZE

I recently read a short essay about breaking free of writer's block. The author expressed how she was energized again and proclaimed, "The goal, to write. The Prize, to publish."

I felt like cheering. To write—yes! A worthy goal. To publish—yes! And it was here that I paused.

The question came to mind—what is the prize? Is it seeing your byline in a magazine or newspaper or on the cover of a book? Is it receiving a cheque for a piece of writing you have laboured over? I've had the thrill of all of these, and yes, it is a thrill, but it is fleeting. The byline may not be noticed nor remembered. The cheque evaporates like mist. Surely there is more.

Is the prize perhaps the process itself? Is the prize all that is learned along the way? Is the prize the life being lived as a writer who belongs to Christ? Is it discovering that your words have made a difference?

Henri Nouwen wrote, "Writing is a process in which we discover what lives in us. The writing itself reveals to us what is alive in us. The deepest satisfaction of writing is precisely that it opens up new spaces within us of which we were not aware before we started to write. To write is to embark on a journey whose final destination we do not know." †

What lives within us—that which is alive—is revealed to us as we write. As those spaces open up within us, we discover Who will fill them. As we trust Him, not knowing the destination becomes irrelevant. He knows the beginning and the end of our stories and our lives.

What greater prize can there be? When we focus on the Spirit of God as the giver and sustainer of the gift, it is as we write that we understand Who that Spirit is. It is as we build our stories, our articles, our poems, that we discover the depth of His wisdom and love.

That journey, that adventure is in itself a gift. I would own no other prize.

† https://henrinouwen.org/meditations/writing-reveals-what-is-alive-in-us

Have you celebrated the journey you are on as a writer?

_____

_____

_____

_____

_____

_____

_____

_____

_____

_____

_____

_____

_____

_____

_____

_____

_____

_____

_____

_____

_____

_____

_____

_____

_____

A WRITER'S EASTER

All over the world during Easter week, writers sit at their computers, staring at a blank monitor or the empty pages in a notebook as they contemplate and struggle to articulate what Easter means. I am one of those writers.

There are many things I know about Easter. I know it is the most important celebration in the Christian calendar. I know without Easter there is no effectual Christianity. I know about the cross, that torturous mode of execution that has become a universal symbol of hope. And I know about the tomb. I've stood inside one in Jerusalem and stared at the rough ledge where they believe our Saviour might have lain, wrapped in grave cloths, waiting for the third day.

But I'm a writer. I want to know more about this drama. I want to get inside the characters' heads. I want to feel Mary's pain and confusion, or perhaps peace, when they arrested her son and dragged him away. I want to know Peter's horror and self-loathing when he ran from the courtyard after denying he knew his Friend, his Saviour, his God. I want to know his catharsis when he answered the same question three times: "Peter, do you love me?"

I want to know how Joseph of Arimathea summoned the courage to openly admit his allegiance to the Christ and petition for his body. I want to know the bloom of understanding when Jesus appeared in the midst of his trembling disciples and said, "Peace, my peace I give to you." I want to know the depth of that profound comprehension when Thomas touched the wound proving the death of his Messiah, and when the two disciples on the road to Emmaus watched Him break the bread before their eyes.

And above all, I want to know the main character in the drama of Easter. I want to know that Messiah. I want to look into his face and know the depth of his knowledge of me and the incomparable love that made him drag himself to that cross as though it were his only source of life. Because He is my only source of life.

I am a writer. I am a believer in this Saviour, Jesus Christ. I count it a privilege to engage in this struggle to understand, to know more and more and more about this drama and all it means. I count it a blessing that there is no end to the understanding of it, as there is no end to the magnificence of God. I am humbled to my core when I contemplate the gift he has given me as I am obedient to the call and struggle to articulate the story.

I pray for all of us this Easter, that need to know drives us to our knees, drives us to His word and drives us to a deeper understanding of the meaning of the words, "He is Risen. He is risen indeed." Glory! Glory Hallelujah!

Have you stared at a blank page and then been totally blessed by what God gave you to write?

_____

_____

_____

_____

_____

_____

_____

_____

_____

_____

_____

_____

_____

_____

_____

_____

_____

_____

_____

_____

_____

A WRITER'S OBEDIENCE

A while ago my husband and I were surfing the channels on TV when we happened upon a biography of Henri Nouwen. I was moved by his story, by the humility he learned when he went from being an acclaimed professor and author to a caregiver for a mentally challenged adult at L'Arche Daybreak Community in Montreal.

And I was struck by Jean Vanier's words. "Henri's call was not just to be with Adam or just to care for him, it was to announce him to us, to the world."

That made me think of another story I heard Philip Yancey tell, of how he sometimes felt guilty when his wife would come home after a busy day of helping people and ask him what he'd done that day. His answer—"Well, I found a great adverb!"—made him feel less than adequate.

I've had those same feelings from time to time, especially when a member of our congregation looks at me like I'm that two-headed writer who sits at a computer all day and doesn't really "do" anything. It's at those times that Mr. Vanier's words ring with a truth I try not to forget. When I feel misunderstood or even guilty, I remember that there were those in the Bible whose only role was to sit at the King's feet and write down what He did. Those scribes were to announce the King's greatness to their world.

We are to do the same in ours. Just as Henri Nouwen announced the beauty of God in the guise of a disabled man, we are to look for those people, places, things, where God is hidden, and reveal Him. This requires a calm spirit, an eager eye and ear, to see and hear what God is revealing to us.

The best place, the best vantage point from which to do that is sitting at His feet, watching, listening, waiting, and then, writing. To a writer, that is obedience.

Sometimes I envision the Lord taking my chin in his hand and turning my head so I will see what He wants me to record. Sometimes I envision him touching my eyes so they can see, my ears that they can hear.

And then I write.

"Each one should use whatever gift he has received to serve others, faithfully administering God's grace in its various forms" (1 Peter 4:10).

Where have you found God hiding lately?

_____

_____

_____

_____

_____

_____

_____

_____

_____

_____

_____

_____

_____

_____

_____

_____

_____

_____

_____

_____

_____

_____

_____

_____

_____

_____

_____

ALL WE HAVE TO DO

The voice coming out of the speaker was clipped and rapid. "What kind of muffin would you like? We have carrot or fat-wise carrot, blueberry or fat-wise blueberry."

My husband and I fell into a fit of giggles. Fat-wise? As we waited at the second window for the goods to be delivered, he joked, "I wonder if it talks? If it's wise, it must be able to talk. What do you think a wise muffin would say?"

"I only care about the fat part," I replied. "A nice plump muffin. Yup, that's what I want."

The muffin was, in fact, small, heavy as a stone, and decidedly mute. As we pulled away from the fast-food restaurant, my husband continued his banter about fat-wise muffins until my daughter groaned and asked him to quit. He shook his head. "I feel for people trying to learn English."

Sometimes the way we use words makes no sense. This seems to be particularly true in advertising. For instance, consider the expressions "jeans your skin" and "my bottoms are tops" or "lips that don't quit" and "two thumbs fresh." Our culture speaks in slogans and metaphors, not to mention anagrams. It's no wonder we laugh at the poster that reads, "I know you believe you understand what you think I said, but I'm not sure you realize that what you heard is not what I meant."

Words can obscure understanding even when intentions are pure. Words can twist meaning when intentions are evil. There are, however, words which can be trusted, words meant to heal and bless. Psalm 12:6 says, "And the words of the Lord are flawless, like silver refined in a furnace of clay, purified seven times."

Isaiah 55:10-11 says, "As the rain and the snow come down from heaven, and do not return to it without watering the earth and making it bud and flourish, so that it yields seed for the sower and bread for the eater, so is my word that goes out from my mouth; it will not return to me empty, but will accomplish what I desire and achieve the purpose for which I sent it."

What words are these? Words of assurance and comfort, words of challenge and reproach, words of guidance and warning, words that nourish and heal. Our culture lives by the words of advertisers and slogan writers, words meant to spin the coin out of our pockets. God's words are meant to give truth, life, peace. As writers we are charged to do likewise, to imitate Christ in this, as in all things. This can at once free us and bind us. The responsibility can sometimes overwhelm, but the good news is that we are not alone. He is guiding our minds and our hearts and when we yield to Him, the outpouring will be words of life and blessing. The good news is that He has purpose for our words, too, and those purposes will be accomplished by His Spirit, to His glory. The good news is, it's not up to us. All we have to do is write.

What do you think God's purpose is for your writing?

_____

_____

_____

_____

_____

_____

_____

_____

_____

_____

_____

_____

_____

_____

_____

_____

_____

_____

_____

_____

_____

AN ACT OF GOD, AN ACT OF GRACE

The day was bright and sunny with just a touch of crispness to it. It was the kind of morning that should have lifted my spirits, but as I gazed out the window my thoughts were far away and all gloomy. I sighed and tried to prepare for the day ahead. I knew it wasn't going to be an easy one.

There would be the gathering of friends and family at the church and then the funeral and a reception immediately afterward. My friend's death had been a shock to us all. As I got ready, I prayed that the Lord would help us get through the day.

I heard the birds as I was eating breakfast. At first, I didn't pay much attention. There was a large tract of bush on the other side of our street, so we heard the birds every morning. But by the time I was ready to head out our front door, I was wondering why the birdsong was so loud. As I stepped out into the fresh spring air, I was astonished at the reason. The entire bush, every branch on every tree across from me, was full of robins. They flitted from branch to branch and tree to tree, singing. I stood and watched and listened and suddenly my spirit was lifted. A verse of scripture that can sometimes seem so impossible came to mind. "My grace is sufficient for you" (2 Corinthians 12:9). I was witnessing an act of grace, a gift given in reply to a plea for help. The gift worked wonders.

I don't know if robins usually move about in large flocks. Perhaps it's part of their migration pattern, but I have never seen a flock like that before, or since. Like many people I've always looked for that single robin that heralds the coming of spring. I would never have dreamed of looking for a flock of hundreds.

Perhaps God knew that's what I needed that day—something unusual and delightful, something that would take my breath away. As I drove to the church, I realized that it's just like Him to do something like that. He has said that He does not only want to give us life, but He wants to give us abundant life, a life full of delightful things like birdsong, to banish the gloom, a life in which the darkness of death is overcome by the blazing light of life.

"Now to Him who is able to do immeasurably more than all we ask or imagine, according to his power that is at work within us, to him be glory in the church and in Christ Jesus throughout all generations, forever and ever! Amen" (Ephesians 3:20).

When has God blessed you in an unexpected way?

_____
_____
_____
_____
_____
_____
_____
_____
_____
_____
_____
_____
_____
_____
_____
_____
_____
_____
_____
_____
_____
_____
_____
_____

_AN APPROPRIATE QUOTE

I read the email with a bit of anticipation and a bit of dread. It was an invitation to yet another Christmas party. That meant another potluck item to prepare, another auction gift to bring. And I couldn't stop sneezing and coughing, so who knew if I'd even be well enough to attend? It was almost enough to make me want to shout, "Bah humbug!"

But the instructions in this email were intriguing and piqued my interest. For the gift exchange, we were to bring a favourite quote, done up in some kind of creative way. The favourite quote part would be easy, I thought. I have a huge file of quotes on my computer. With the state of my health, I knew the creative part might be a bit more difficult, but I decided to try and rise to the challenge.

I clicked into my quotes file and began to read, and read, and read. Nothing seemed exactly right. I was thinking Christmas but couldn't find anything seasonal. I thought inspirational, but nothing seemed to hit the mark. I thought humorous but couldn't find anything that made me laugh out loud. So I gave up, swallowed some more cough medicine and went to bed.

The next day I opened the file again. A quote seemed to beam its way to me immediately. It was short but thought provoking, and when I thought about it, the words from poet Anne Sexton were very appropriate for the Christmas season: "Put your ear down close to your soul and listen hard."

In the midst of the rush to shop, to bake, to decorate, and to make it to all those Christmas parties, God is calling us to do just that. He wants us to stop and hear His voice in the tumult. It is a still small voice, but one that echoes with everything we need. It is the voice of a child crying from a manger, the voices of angels singing and shepherds jabbering about a baby born to be King. It is a voice weeping for those in pain and sickness. It is a voice mourning for those who refuse to hear Him. It is a voice shouting victory over the forces of evil and death. And it is a voice calling us to know Him, to know His love for us, love that grants us one more day of life filled with all its challenges and blessings.

Listen for Him. He has promised that anyone "who hears my voice and opens the door, I will come in and eat with him, and he with me" (Revelation 3:20). So, "put your ear down close to your soul and listen hard." You might just hear the true voice of Christmas.

What have you heard?

_____

_____

_____

_____

_____

_____

_____

_____

_____

_____

_____

_____

_____

_____

_____

_____

_____

_____

_____

_____

_____

_____

_____

_____

_____

AN EXCITING DISCOVERY

I made an exciting discovery one day. I got so excited about it I called my husband into the office so I could show him. He smiled indulgently but looked like he thought I was overreacting just a bit. I'd been critiquing and editing manuscripts for writers for some time. I would usually do the edits on a hard copy of the manuscript, then transfer them onto the computer and send the finished product to the writer. The task was laborious since it is important for the writer to see the changes I make and, in some cases, understand my reasoning. I used the highlight feature as well as the font color feature on the computer, making the changes as I went, then highlighting and putting comments in red. This required continually clicking buttons and using the mouse.

Then I joined an online critique group. Each person was to submit a story and all the others critique it. As we got started someone asked how to put the changes right into the manuscript. I was about to send a message explaining my method when I read a message from another group member. He explained that all you have to do is hit the Tools button and click on "Track Changes." The computer does everything for you! I immediately pulled up an old manuscript and tried it. That's when I got excited. I knew this little discovery would save me a lot of time and "fiddling."

In my own defense I must explain that I am self-taught on the computer. I have never taken a course but learned by doing. For the most part that has worked fine, but when I discovered this tracking feature it made me wonder what else I've been missing. Maybe it's time I investigated all the features the program designers put into my computer. Maybe it's time I discovered how it's meant to be used. There are probably a few other things I've been doing the hard way.

Sometimes we go through life the same way. We are self-made, self-taught and self-focused. Usually, that means we've been doing things the hard way. Maybe it's time we discovered our designer had a different plan. Maybe it's time we discovered what that plan is. God has provided everything we need to live our lives according to His purposes. The Apostle Paul knew this when he wrote to the Philippians, "And my God will meet all your needs according to his glorious riches in Christ Jesus" (Philippians 4:19).

Did you notice that last phrase? That's the important part, the part that can mean the difference between living life the hard way and living life with abundant joy. "In Christ Jesus." Why do things the hard way?

Have you been doing things the hard way?

AN INVITATION

Someone once asked me, if I wasn't a writer what would I do? I immediately thought of all the wonderful creative pursuits I'd love to indulge in. I paint a little and would love to do more. My mind sometimes seems to work like a camera, so I'd love to pursue being a photographer. My daughter has made me cry when she danced, and I'd give a lot to be able to move to music like she does. And music—oh my, to play the piano or guitar or—well, I could go on and on. I can think of a lot of things to do, and I think many of them would satisfy my need to create.

But I am a writer.

Thoreau wrote, "We are continually invited to become who we are." I believe I am continually invited to become a writer. But sometimes I find that path hard. It takes determined effort and no small amount of discipline. Sometimes it seems a heavy burden. Sometimes I wish I could do anything else other than write.

It need not be so. When I trust in the God who continually invites me to be the child he created me to be, faith grows. When I draw close to Him, the effort and struggle slip away. In those moments I move into that wonderful state called grace. In those moments writing becomes a state of being rather than a state of doing.

Eugene Patterson's paraphrase puts it like this: "Get away with me and you'll recover your life. I'll show you how to take a real rest. Walk with me and work with me—watch how I do it. Learn the unforced rhythms of grace. I won't lay anything heavy or ill-fitting on you. Keep company with me and you'll learn to live freely and lightly" (Matthew 11:28-30, The Message).

God continually invites us to become what He created us to be, His children, designed to live a life of joy and abundance, savouring His grace and mercy. He has opened the way to achieve that by giving us all a creative process, a framework within which to work, a unique way of keeping company with Him.

No matter what you are invited to become, the invitation to do it joyfully with Him is always there.

How are you ensuring that you are becoming
who you are meant to be?

_____

_____

_____

_____

_____

_____

_____

_____

_____

_____

_____

_____

_____

_____

_____

_____

_____

_____

_____

_____

_____

_____

AN ORDINARY THING

I love the book of Exodus, especially chapters 4 and 5. I love the way God used an ordinary thing—a shepherd's staff—to reveal Himself to Moses and Aaron and the people who watched.

God made that ordinary thing into a divine instrument. It was a tool that became a concrete symbol of God's presence and God's power and His desire to communicate with those who would dare to wield an instrument of His choosing. Each miracle Moses and Aaron performed before Pharaoh and the Israelites was done with the staff in hand and was the means by which the people learned about God. It was also the means by which Aaron and Moses learned about Him.

I believe we writers have been given a tool, an instrument as ordinary as that shepherd's staff. God wants us to use it to set His people free, to His glory. Just as God gave Moses his staff, He has given us the gift of language that we might both speak and listen, that we might both teach and learn. He has given us the gift of the written language to show that He is present with us and to reveal His power. He has given these gifts to show us the depth of His love and His desire for communion with His people.

Like Moses, we may want to run from the amazing things God will do with His instrument. Like Moses, we may show signs of false humility and say, "My talent isn't that big; I don't expect to do such great things for God." We must learn it is not what we will do for God, but what God wants to do and will do through us when we are willing.

Like Moses, we must trust our God enough to pick up the snake by the tail. We must wield the instrument He has given us with faith and expectancy, coming before His throne boldly with the confidence that comes from knowing we belong to Him, knowing He will never spurn His own children.

The gift of language is God's instrument in our hands. May we use it wisely with humility and grace, to His glory.

What have you done with the gift of language?

_____

_____

_____

_____

_____

_____

_____

_____

_____

_____

_____

_____

_____

_____

_____

_____

_____

_____

_____

_____

_____

_____

_____

_____

_____

AN UNEXPECTED ATTACK

My husband trained as a radio technician in the air force but was also trained as part of the base's defense force. That meant, during the periodic "war games," his assignment was to guard the end of the runway in the event of an "enemy" attack. He was alone, with only the standard issue rifle for the job. He was usually "killed" very early in the exercise. My husband admitted that his assignment was ridiculous. "Had there been a real enemy," he said, "I wouldn't have been a deterrent, I would have been a target."

When I heard that story, I immediately thought, "Duh, what were they thinking?" But then I realized the games those soldiers played back then were just that. They were games with no expectation of a real attack. There had been no 9/11. An attack on North American soil was unthinkable. When you don't expect an enemy to attack, you don't bother taking precautions.

I fell into that trap when I was close to finishing the final draft of my novel, *One Smooth Stone*. I hit one of those well-known walls that writers often do. It's a wall that screams back at you. "This book will never go anywhere! It's not worth publishing! Who said you could write? Who do you think you are?"

I'd forgotten that in the war being waged all around us, the work God has given me to do will make me a target. Too often we don't expect the enemy of our souls to attack. Perhaps we feel secure in our good works—all the work we've produced to date that have told us we're doing just fine. When we fall into that trap, we are like my husband, alone with a very small weapon and, like him, we'll be "dead" before the "game" has hardly begun.

The Bible says that our enemy "prowls around like a roaring lion looking for someone to devour. Resist him, standing firm in the faith" (1Peter 5:8-9). How do we resist an enemy set on our destruction? First, know that he will attack. Then arm ourselves with the knowledge of God, the knowledge of His Word, and of His promises that will never be broken. Promises like the one that tells us He is our protector and our refuge. Promises that tell us that His purposes for us, and our work, will not fail. The enemy can't roar loud enough to make a difference when we are listening and responding to God's voice. Then we know we will never stand alone.

In the spiritual battles of life, there is far more at stake than the defense of a military base, far more than the defense of an entire nation. The battle is for our eternal souls. With stakes that high, we must expect the attack and always be on the alert.

What do you do when you experience the enemy's attack?

_____

_____

_____

_____

_____

_____

_____

_____

_____

_____

_____

_____

_____

_____

_____

_____

_____

_____

_____

_____

_____

_____

_____

_____

AN UNPLEASANT THOUGHT

W.O. Mitchell is quoted as saying, "The most constant state of an artist is uncertainty. You must face confusion, self-questioning, dilemma. Only amateurs are confident ... be prepared to live with the fear of failure all your art life."

Not a pleasant thought, is it? As writers, we all live with some uncertainty. We write an article and never really know its worth until someone reads it and makes comment. We stew about that book manuscript, wondering if any editor will think it worthy of publishing. We spend hours polishing a poem and wonder if we have wasted our time. We will, from time to time, face confusion, self-questioning and even dilemma, as Mitchell suggests, but we do not have to live in that state.

The writer of Hebrews told his readers that they, too, would face uncertainty, confusion, dilemma. They would face persecution and, yes, the appearance of failure. Then he said, "So do not throw away your confidence; it will be richly rewarded. You need to persevere so that when you have done the will of God, you will receive what he has promised" (Hebrews 10:35-36). The writer of Hebrews is not talking about the self-confidence of a much-published writer, which can lead to pride and an overblown ego. He is talking about the confidence "to enter the Most Holy Place."

The reference here is to the inner sanctuary, the place where only a high priest could enter, and only once a year after much preparation. Even then, the priest risked death when he stepped on that holy ground. For there, there in that place, was God. And how is it we can have such audacity, to enter with confidence? "[B]y the blood of Jesus" (Hebrews 10:19).

A writer who is Christian does not have to submit to a perspective like Mitchell's. As believers, we can have confidence, not in our own talents but in the fact that God is there. He is approachable and accessible, and He has promised to use our gifts and talents to serve others, to His glory. Therefore, there is no need for fear of failure nor of success. Our confidence is in Christ. Our calling is to work in obedience and humility.

The writer of Hebrews continues: "Let us hold unswervingly to the hope we profess, for he who promised is faithful. And let us consider how we may spur one another on toward love and good deeds." As writers, we have all been given a spur—the gift of communication—to use for the sake of others and for the sake of our most faithful God. May He find us faithful to that task.

How are you ensuring that you put your confidence in Christ?

_____

_____

_____

_____

_____

_____

_____

_____

_____

_____

_____

_____

_____

_____

_____

_____

_____

_____

_____

_____

_____

_____

_____

_____

_____

_____

BAD NEWS/GOOD NEWS

I attended a seminar recently put on by the Writers' Union of Canada. The first presenter was obviously very savvy about all that is currently going on in the publishing world. At first the changes he outlined were rather discouraging. He stated there are now fewer opportunities for emerging writers in the traditional publishing spheres, and even established writers are finding it hard to get their next book into print. Editing is no longer done by many houses, leaving it up to the authors to make sure their work is polished, at their own expense. Mid-range publishers are having a hard time staying afloat, and at every turn the bottom line is paramount.

It would seem that publishing is no longer driven by the quality of the manuscript but by the marketing department. A "platform" is mandatory for all authors, and they have to present a solid marketing plan of their own before a publishing house will consider their work. Add to that all the changes that are happening due to the world wide web, and things look unstable at best. The instructor quoted an agent who lamented, "The sky is falling and the ground is shifting all at the same time."

But then he smiled and began to talk excitedly about the opportunities these changes are opening up for writers of all kinds all over the world. He showed us clips from YouTube and examples of web pages and blogs where people are doing creative things and even making some money while doing it. Then he said something that made me smile. "Freedom for writers today means finding joy in the turbulence."

I like that perspective. Instead of moaning about all the changes and fearing the future, we can jump in and enjoy it as we adapt and learn and reach out to the world. Never before have we been able to reach so many people so easily and quickly. Never before has there been so much potential for creativity and free expression.

As writers who are Christian, I believe finding "joy in the turbulence" is particularly apt. Who better to smile at the chaos than those who know there is One who stands firm and unchanging? Who better to embrace the changes than those who recognize the world is illusory and true reality lies beyond? Who better to step up and engage the world with all the creativity we have been blessed with than those who know its source?

Some have said the changes in the publishing industry can be compared to the invention of the first printing press. That event changed the world. The current events are taking us into worlds we didn't even know could exist. I wonder, what amazing things does God have in store for us all as we leap into them? "Joy in the turbulence." Amen.

Recount a time when you found joy in the turbulence.

_____

_____

_____

_____

_____

_____

_____

_____

_____

_____

_____

_____

_____

_____

_____

_____

_____

_____

_____

_____

_____

_____

_____

_____

BORROWED WORDS

"When you were out in the workforce, where did your paycheck come from?"

I frowned at the teacher and immediately thought of my previous employer. As a first-year student in Bible College and a brand new Christian, I thought it was a ridiculous question, not the stuff to stimulate deep spiritual thought.

The professor gave us a moment, then said, "If you're thinking of an employer, you're wrong. Your paychecks came from God and they belong to God."

I was stunned. Of course, he was absolutely right. That point marked a dramatic shift in how I thought about everything I considered "mine."

Too often I think of the words I tap out on my computer as mine, especially when I have worked hard for them, when I've rewritten and edited and reedited until I'm absolutely certain it's right. I claim it for my own. But it all belongs to God—every word.

There is a wonderful old hymn about Christ's suffering and death called "O Sacred Head, Now Wounded." It is often sung during the Easter season, and I've often been moved by it, but singing it once in the company of a group of writers gave the last verse new meaning for me, especially these words: "What language shall I borrow to thank Thee, dearest Friend, for this, Thy dying sorrow, Thy pity without end?"

When I sang those words the reality of God's gift to us amazed me. Our very language is borrowed from God! He gave it to us that we might use it to glorify Him. As I sang the words of that hymn, it struck me again, what an awesome responsibility we have as the stewards of language and of words. We are the borrowers, the users, but not the owners.

If we are true to that stewardship, we must acknowledge the struggle of life and of faith by using words we have struggled with, to convey it. I have become aware of this in my own writing in the past while, especially in my poetry. I've always put poetry in a "second class citizen" category. Poetry has been something I've done when the mood strikes me, something I did not take very seriously. But God has impressed on me that I have no right to relegate any words to a second-class level. They are God's gift. I am in grave error if I treat them as anything less. We borrow language, words, images, the stuff of writing. It is up to us to acknowledge the original owner, to offer back to Him what we have done with that which we have borrowed and glorify the One who spoke the first word into existence.

"Now it is required that those who have been given a trust must prove faithful" (1Corinthians 4:2).

How are you being true to the stewardship of words?

_____

_____

_____

_____

_____

_____

_____

_____

_____

_____

_____

_____

_____

_____

_____

_____

_____

_____

_____

_____

_____

_____

CARRYING THE CHEESE

I heard a well-known story recently about David, the future king of Israel. As I listened, I pictured David as a young man, eager for adventure, eager to take his place beside his brothers on the battlefield. I wonder if David schemed a bit when his father called him home. I wonder if he didn't fantasize just a little about wearing armor and carrying a sharp sword. Imagine his disappointment when his father placed a donkey's lead in his hand instead. He was not being sent to the front lines to fight the great battle and win the victory. He was being sent to give nourishment to those who were fighting.

Perhaps David's cry to God went like this: "But Lord, You've given me strength enough to kill lions and bears. You had the prophet anoint me king. So why, Lord? Why do you ask me to only carry the cheese?"

Yet David obeyed. It was later he discovered that submitting to the role of the servant was God's way of putting him where he would do the most good. God did have bigger things planned, and David's journey to get there was part of his preparation for an even bigger picture. God was making David not just into the boy-hero who slew the giant, but into a King worthy of his anointing.

Sometimes writers dream and scheme as David did. We know our gifts; we see the needs and are eager to do great things. But often the path God tells us to walk does not seem to lead to the place where we think we would do the most good. We would do well to remember that God knows the bigger picture. He knows the plans He has for us, "plans for good and not for disaster, to give you a future and a hope" (Jeremiah 29:11). Like David, we are being shaped into useful tools. And like David we are best shaped when we are serving others.

Is there a donkey's lead dangling in front of you? Perhaps God is telling you to get up and carry some cheese.

How have you reacted when you've been called to carry the cheese?

_____

_____

_____

_____

_____

_____

_____

_____

_____

_____

_____

_____

_____

_____

_____

_____

_____

_____

_____

_____

_____

_____

CHANGING THE WORLD

"If you have changed a life, you have changed the world."

My head jerked up when I heard that sentence. It was at InScribe's Fall Conference and our speaker, Kathleen Gibson, was doing a great job of speaking to the hearts of all the writers there. But that one sentence really hit me. I'd thought about changing lives before. I've had emails and letters and even phone calls telling me that God has done exactly that through the words I've put on paper. But changing the world? Really?

Then I thought about another speaker we'd had at one of our conferences. He told us that not very far back in his family line, someone read a book and became a believer in Christ. He told us that now there are many branches to his family, and many are preachers of God's word, missionaries, and others serving in their churches across North America. None of it would have happened, but for one book.

I began to consider all the ripple effects that one book has had—not just in the lives of his family members but in all the lives they have touched. I thought about the book I was given just as God was softening my heart toward him. It was a copy of Josh McDowell's *Evidence that Demands a Verdict*. It was put into my hands at exactly the perfect time. It convinced my head that Jesus was who He claimed to be—the Son of God, a man who came to earth to change the world by changing each one of us.

And I was stunned into awe and gratitude for what the Holy Spirit did in my life through that book. Words are such small things. They can be simple or profound, plain or eloquent. But when God takes them and bends them to His purposes, He changes hearts with them and those hearts change the lives of others and those touch others and on and on.

Who knows how far our words will go. If you have changed a life, you have changed the world.

Yes. Really.

Do you believe you can change the world? Recount a time when you read something that changed you.

COMMITMENT AND PROVIDENCE

Until one is committed, there is hesitancy, the chance to draw back, always ineffectiveness. Concerning all acts of initiative there is one elemental truth, the ignorance of which kills countless ideas and splendid plans: that moment one definitely commits oneself, then Providence moves too. All sorts of things occur to help that would never have otherwise occurred. A whole stream of events issues from the decision, raising in one's favor all manner of unforeseen incidents, meetings, and material assistance which no man or woman would have dreamed could have come his way. Whatever you can do, or dream you can do, begin it. Boldness has genius, power, and magic to it. Begin it now. (Goethe)

Let's play "What If."

What if Abram didn't pull up the tent pegs and set off from Ur?

What if Noah didn't pick up the hammer?

What if Moses didn't pick up the staff?

What if Gideon didn't climb out of the winepress and break down the altar to Baal?

What if Joshua didn't march around Jericho?

What if Ruth didn't go with Naomi?

What if David didn't take the provisions to his brothers on the front lines?

What if Solomon didn't build the temple?

What if Shaphan the secretary didn't read the book of the Law to Josiah?

What if Josiah didn't tear his robes?

What if Esther stayed home?

What if Daniel didn't pay attention to his dreams?

What if Matthew didn't walk away from the tax collector's booth?

What if Peter didn't put down his nets?

What if you don't take up your pen?

Are you up for the challenge? What if you don't take up your pen?

_____

_____

_____

_____

_____

_____

_____

_____

_____

_____

_____

_____

_____

_____

_____

_____

_____

_____

_____

_____

_____

_____

_____

_____

A THING CALLED GROG

Some people seem to have an underlying belief that writing about what is painful and ugly in life is somehow denying the goodness of God. I disagree. We do not write about the ugly, the dark things in order to glorify them, nor to question God, but in order to put them in their place and to recognize that there is something more: there is redemption, because of what happened on a cross at the base of a hill in a tiny country then called Palestine.

Psalm 12:6 says, "The words of the Lord are pure words: as silver tried in a furnace of earth, purified seven times" (KJV). "Tried in a furnace of earth." That doesn't sound pleasant to me. "Purified seven times." That sounds like struggle and anguish and pain that has been *forged* into what is pure and wholesome.

As a pottery student, I learned that you can't use just any old clay to make pottery. It has to be the right consistency, the right combination of elements. Some clay is too fine. When it's thrown on a wheel it won't stand up, or it won't survive the heat of the kiln, so a substance called grog is added. Grog is clay that has been previously fired in the kiln, then ground into fine particles. Grog sometimes hurts. As you throw a pot on the wheel you can feel it scraping your hands. Sometimes it even makes them bleed.

Our writing needs grog—that stuff that has been ground up inside us as we struggle. We must put the stuff of real life into it, or it won't hold up. It won't do what it is intended to do. I wrote this short devotional for a local paper some time ago. I called it "Hard Questions":

> It seemed fitting that the sky hung heavy and low. It seemed right that the wind was bitter, howling with the fierce shriek of winter around a tiny country cemetery. There was a very small hole in the ground and a very tiny casket to be put into it. It seemed appropriate that we all stood numbed by the cold of that day.
>
> A friend of mine once wrote a poem about Adam, Eve, and God in the Garden of Eden. It was a good poem, well-constructed with a strong rhythm and powerful images. One of those images often comes to mind when bad things happen to good people. It's an image of God curled into a fetal position, and the wailing sound of His weeping.
>
> Sometimes we ask hard questions. Why did that baby have to die, God? Why is my friend suffering with a painful cancer? Why are those people in Africa starving? We don't usually get a good answer to those questions. They leave us numb and they leave us wondering if God is there.

But then there is that image and that sound. In my friend's poem God mourned the first disobedience, the first break in His relationship with the creatures He put on the earth.

The picture my friend painted with his words was of a God who cares, a God who feels our pain, a God who mourns with us, especially at the graves of tiny babies.

He is also a God who will answer. He is a God who acted to redeem all that was broken in our world. He is a God who continues to do so. The redemption was accomplished on the cross of Calvary, but it is not yet complete. As the writer of the book of Hebrews said, God "waits for his enemies to be made his footstool, because by one sacrifice he has made perfect forever those who are being made holy" (Hebrews 10:13).

The process is sometimes painful, but the world will one day be made entirely new, entirely redeemed. The scriptures talk about creation groaning as we wait for that day. The groans do not fall on deaf ears, nor will they remain unanswered forever. One day that tiny baby will rise, whole and perfect as God intended him to be.

God's plan is unfolding. What then, should we do in those times when we groan and feel there is no answer? Again, scripture tells us "to act justly, to love mercy and to walk humbly with your God" (Micah 6:8).

Humility before God bows the knee and continues to believe. Humility before God acknowledges His sovereignty and calls Him good. Even when babies die and the pain of this world overwhelms, humility before God says, "Blessed be the name of the Lord."

The Sunday after that piece appeared in print, the father of that baby approached me in the lobby of our church. He said he was in a local restaurant when he read "Hard Questions." He said it wasn't long before tears were streaming down his face. I held my breath as he described what he was feeling. Many things flew through my mind. Was he angry with me? Should I have written and published that piece when it exposed not only my pain, but his?

Then, with tears brimming in his eyes he said, "Thank you. It was part of the healing. Thank you for writing it."

Madeleine L'Engle has said, "The discipline of creation, be it to paint, compose, write, is an effort toward wholeness." This is our responsibility— to struggle toward that wholeness in our lives and in our work; to take our work deeper, to make sure it has enough grog in it to stand, and perhaps even to heal. All to the glory of God, because that is His plan for us, His plan for our work.

How can you ensure that your work has enough grog in it?

_____

_____

_____

_____

_____

_____

_____

_____

_____

_____

_____

_____

_____

_____

_____

_____

_____

_____

_____

_____

_____

_____

_____

A Note from Marcia

I hope you enjoyed working through this journal. If you did there is good news—there is another volume to enjoy! To order contact Marcia at vinemarc@telus.net

And have a look at my other books—adult novels, fantasy novels, devotionals—on my website, https://marcialeelaycock.com, and online at Amazon and Smashwords.

One more thing—if you have appreciated this book, please take a moment to leave a review on Amazon.ca and com and on any other platforms you frequent.

With thanks, and blessings,
Marcia

About the Author

Marcia Lee Laycock is an award-winning writer and sought-after speaker. Her devotional books, *Spur of the Moment* and *Celebrate This Day* are available on her website, https://marcialeelaycock.com

Marcia was the winner of the Best New Canadian Christian Author Award for her novel, *One Smooth Stone*. The sequel, *A Tumbled Stone*, was also shortlisted for an award and her fantasy novel, *Journey to a Strong Tower* (under pen-name M.C. Spencer) was the winner of a Word Award from Write!Canada.

Her work has been endorsed by notable Christian authors, including Janette Oke, Sigmund Brouwer, Phil Callaway and Mark Buchanan.

Marcia lives in Alberta, Canada with her retired pastor husband, Spence and a Bernedoodle named Livy. She is also the mother of three grown daughters and mother-in-law to two great sons and grandmother to two brilliant grandkids.

www.ingramcontent.com/pod-product-compliance
Lightning Source LLC
Chambersburg PA
CBHW071542120626
46550CB00006B/2552